It was a beautiful sunny day to go to the park. My friend and I rode our bikes there with my sunflower placed in the front of my bike. We rode around until we found a place to lay our picnic basket. Finally, we saw a shaded area where we could sit and have something to eat. I grabbed my sunflower and placed it in water. I felt that today was my lucky day. We were on our way to a great start.

We have a lot of places to go. we have our shoes on our feet and places to see. We can go in any direction we choose. After we finish eating. And you know where you want to go first. And you can guide yourself by that big yellow sunflower sign.

You'll need to look in every direction before you cross that busy street. You'll need to make sure you look up and down before you cross the street. You have your sunflower map. And you have your favorite yellow sneakers on your feet. You have an idea of what you want to do first. So off you go!

Whatever you do, don't
forget your sunflower in
that cup. Cause I don't

want to come back and help you look for it. I won't forget it. I go everywhere with my sunflower. My sunflower is my lucky charm. It brightens up my day everytime. Now where to next?

You may not be able to find me for a while. I haven't been to this park in so long. I want to explore everything. You'll want to go down because that's where the water rides are. I ,myself, will go straight to see the sunflowers up the road. Off I go!

What a huge sunflower field with lots of beautiful sunflowers! I've never seen such beautiful sunflowers in this park. This is a beautiful day to pick out sunflowers. The sun is out and shining bright. There's different things happening all around us ,people to see and things to do.

Now, what's that? Is that a puppy I see? It's heading towards me. I'm not scared of a puppy. I'll just pat it on it's head and go on my merry way. Now how many sunflower will I choose today. I'm off to pick my sunflowers.

"Oh! The places you'll go to pick out sunflower's", I thought to myself. I'm picking out sunflowers and it's a beautiful sunny day. I wanted to take all of them.

Oh! How I love sunflowers! I felt like I was floating on air. Wow! It was a beautiful day indeed to pick out sunflowers.

As I ride through the park, everywhere I go, people stop and stare. And say, "Why your sunflowers are so beautiful?" I felt so good inside. When I heard them say that. I realized that I'm not the only one that loves sunflowers. There's other people that do too.

Finally, I have my sunflowers in my hands. I must go and look for Sonny. I saw him from afar. I am going to run to catch up with him. I ran so fast. I bumped into him. We tumbled to the ground and I scraped my knees. My sunflowers all fell to the ground and Sonny helped me pick them up.

How many of these sunflowers do you have? I have too many to count. That's a lot. So, Sunny began to count them as he picked them off the ground. Before he could finish counting them, I yelled out,"I have ten sunflowers!" Wow! That's a lot of sunflowers for one girl. I know. I love sunflowers. Sunflowers are my favorite flowers in the whole world.

Without much more to do, Sonny and I rode our bikes back home. With all of my sunflowers placed in front of my bike, we raced home. We had a great time today at the park, didn't we? Yes, we did. I must say sunflowers really put a smile on your face Mally. I love the way they make you feel. I do too. I feel great. I think tomorrow I am going to plant my own sunflowers in the backyard so I can have them all year round. That sounds like a great idea. I'll visit you tomorrow and we can plant them together. Great! See you tomorrow , Sonny.